The Nature in Close-up Series

Grewcock, David
    Deer.——(Nature in close-up)
    1. Deer——Juvenile literature
    I. Title   II. Series
    599.73'57   QL737.U55
    ISBN 0–7136–2592–9

Published by A & C Black (Publishers) Limited
35 Bedford Row, London WC1R 4JH

First published 1985
© 1985 David Grewcock

ISBN 0-7136-2592-9

Filmset by August Filmsetting, Haydock, St Helens.
Printed in Hong Kong by Dai Nippon Printing Co. Ltd

Nature in Close-up

DEER

David Grewcock

To Helen Charlotte.

David C. Grewcock

A & C Black · London

Contents

Introduction

How many different kinds of deer can you think of?
Around the world, there are over forty different
species. The red deer on this page are just one of
the kinds of deer which live in this country.

The male red deer is called a *stag*. The female is
called a *hind*. For most of the year, it's easy to tell
them apart because the stag grows large, branched
horns, called antlers. Hinds do not grow antlers.

This book will tell you about red deer and how they
live in the wild. It will also tell you about other
types of deer and how you can recognise them.

Red deer stag and hind ▶

Tracks and signs

Here are some of the ways you can tell that red deer are nearby.

Red deer often have favourite places for feeding and mating and use the same paths over and over again. Look out for these well-worn paths, which are called *racks*.

If you find a rack, you may be able to see some hoof prints left by a red deer. Deer have *cloven* hooves. Cloven means divided into two parts. The hoof prints left by the deer are called *slots*. The slot of a fully grown red deer is about 6 cm across at the heel.

▲ Look out for well-worn paths

Look carefully at the slots. You can find out a lot about the red deer that made them. Young red deer leave slots which are close together. If the slots are deeper and further apart, they have probably been made by a male red deer, which is larger and heavier.

◀ A deer slot

Another sign to look for on the ground are heaps of droppings. Deer droppings are called *crotties* and are quite small – about 1.5 cms long.

Look at the trees and bushes which are growing along a rack. Red deer reach up to eat leaves from low growing branches. Sometimes they leave a *browse line* which shows how far they can reach.

You might find a tree that is used as a *rubbing post*. The bark will be worn smooth where the red deer has rubbed its coat against it. See if there are any hairs caught in the bark. Deer often use the same tree year after year.

The deer might also leave its scent on the tree. Both stags and hinds have *glands* under their eyes and on their legs that make a scent. The deer rubs its head on grass and twigs to leave its scent behind. This warns other animals that the deer is in the neighbourhood.

▼ This bush has a browse line left by deer which have been feeding on the lower branches

▼ Red deer crotties

Red deer in close-up

In the wild, deer are very timid animals. They live on high hills and in forests away from people. If you are lucky enough to visit a park or zoo, where deer are more used to people, you may be able to get quite close to the animals without frightening them away.

Red deer are one of the largest kinds of deer. They are between 100 and 130 cms tall (measuring from the shoulder to the ground). The name red deer comes from the reddish-brown coat of thick, coarse hair.

An older stag with a mane ▶

▲ A stag shedding his winter coat

In autumn, the coat, or *pelage*, grows thicker to protect them against the cold weather. It turns a greyish-brown, often with a black line running from head to tail.

Stags grow extra hair around their neck and shoulders in winter. This is called a *mane*. Older stags keep their mane all the year round. Red deer shed their winter coats again in April to June.

Can you see the creamy-white patch around the red deer's tail? This is called the *target*. The tail itself is the same colour on top as the pelage, and white underneath.

Deer belong to the same family as sheep, cows and goats. All these animals have cloven hooves. Red deer have very long, thin legs to help them run fast. They are good at jumping and swimming, too.

▲ The target is a lighter colour than the pelage

▼ Red deer hind jumping a wall

▲ Stags in velvet

How antlers grow

Deer are the only animals which shed their antlers every year. Other animals, such as cows and goats, have horns which grow longer each year. These animals' horns are made of *keratin*, the same material which our fingernails are made of. Deer antlers are made of bone and are very strong.

The antlers grow from two points on the red deer's forehead. These points are called *pedicles*. The first part of the antler to grow is called the *coronet*. The coronet is wider than the rest of the antler. The main part of the antler grows up from the coronet and curves backward. It is called the *beam*. The branches which grow from the beam are called *points*. Usually a stag grows an extra point on its antlers each year.

9

In late February each year, the older stags shed their antlers. Younger stags keep their antlers for another few weeks. Red deer often chew on fallen antlers. They are full of calcium and other minerals which the animals need to eat. At this time of year you may see deer with only one antler which hasn't yet been shed.

When the antler falls off, it leaves a bony, red patch on the red deer's forehead. In a few days, new antlers begin to grow.

The first signs of the new antlers are small, furry bumps on the forehead. The new antlers grow under a skin called the *velvet*. This helps to protect the antlers while the bone is soft and still growing. Sometimes a red deer injures an antler while it is in velvet. Then the antler grows in an odd shape.

▲ A fallen antler

▼ When the antlers are shed, they leave a red, bony pedicle

▼ Antlers covered with velvet

▲ A stag cleaning his antlers on a
fallen branch

It usually takes about four months for the new antlers to grow and harden. Then the velvet covering dries out and begins to peel away. The stag cleans his new antlers by rubbing them against trees and bushes. This polishes away the velvet and leaves the antler points shining white.

A stag which has plenty of food may grow very large antlers. A five-year-old stag can have as many as twelve points on its antlers. This is known as a *Royal Head*.

As a stag grows older, its antler points usually grow shorter. Sometimes a stag grows antlers with no points. These long, spiky antlers can be very dangerous when they are used for fighting.

◀ Velvet stripping from the antlers

▲ A group of hinds and calves grazing

Feeding

The best time to watch red deer is in the early morning and evening when they are feeding. In quiet places, where they are not likely to be disturbed, red deer might feed during the day.

Red deer are *herbivores*, which means that they only eat plants. Their main food is grass, moss and leaves which they strip from trees and bushes. You might see a stag using its antlers to pull down high branches so that it can eat the leaves.

In autumn, red deer eat acorns, beech nuts, and sweet chestnuts. They also eat ivy leaves, which are poisonous to most other animals. When food is hard to find, deer will eat the bark from conifers. Sometimes they eat farm crops. Red deer which live near the sea might even eat seaweed!

Red deer need special teeth to strip leaves from branches and to chew grass. They have eight front teeth on the bottom jaw, and a pad of hard gum on the top jaw. The front teeth make a very tight fit over the gum. At the back of the mouth, there are special teeth for grinding and chewing. The two longer teeth at the front are called *tushes*.

▲ Hind feeding in woodland

▼ This stag is chewing the cud

In order to get all the goodness from their food, deer need to swallow it more than once. When the deer is grazing, it swallows the partly-chewed food and stores it in the stomach. Later, when the deer is resting, the food is brought up to chew again. This is called *chewing the cud*. You might have seen cows lying in a field chewing the cud. Animals that do this are called *ruminants*. They need four stomachs to eat like this! 13

▲ A red deer hind with one year-
old and two year-old calves
behind her

Family groups

Most of the time, the red deer hinds and stags live
in separate groups.

The hinds and young red deer stay near the
sheltered feeding areas. One of the older hinds
usually becomes the leader of the group. She knows
where to find food all the year round. In autumn,
she finds a safe place for the group to shelter in the
cold weather.

Sometimes a young hind from another group strays into the feeding area. She is quickly driven away by the leader who boxes with her hooves as a warning.

The stags usually live together in groups, though older stags sometimes move around on their own. A younger stag may travel with an older stag, standing guard while the older stag feeds or rests.

There is no real leader in the stag group, but the stags fight each other from time to time to test each other's strength. They clash antlers until one of the stags gives up.

A hind boxing with her hooves ▶

▲ Stag leaving his scent on the grass

The rut

Once a year in October or November, groups of red deer meet together at the *rutting stand*. This is the place where they will mate.

The rutting stand is usually where the hinds live. To get there, stags often travel many miles, crossing roads, jumping high fences and even swimming rivers.

At the rutting stand, each stag marks out an area which will be his *territory*. He does this by rubbing his head and legs on grass and twigs to leave a scent. This will warn other stags and animals not to come too close.

In cold, frosty weather, the stag's scent is less strong, so he roars to warn other males to keep away. This also attracts the hinds. The stags show off by wallowing in muddy pools and crashing their antlers against young trees and shrubs.

▼ Stag roaring at the rut at dawn

▲ Stags fighting with their antlers

Stags of the same size compete for hinds. They often walk side by side for quite long distances, until one of them runs away or turns to fight. The stags fight with their antlers. Sometimes, an antler is broken, or a stag is injured. But usually one of the stags gives up before this happens.

When a stag has gathered up a group, or *parcel*, of hinds he rounds up any strays and brings them back to his rutting stand. Younger stags often try to steal hinds from an older stag. They wait near the edge of a group of hinds. When the older stag is not looking, they run into the middle, scattering the hinds. Then they run off with any hinds which break away from the main group.

When the red deer have mated, the stags and hinds drift into different groups again. But the two groups will stay in the same area until the new red deer are born.

17

Young red deer

During June and July the young red deer calves are born. Early in the morning, the hind finds a quiet place away from the main herd. She lies down among grass, bracken and heather so that her calf will be warm and hidden.

The new-born calf weighs about 7 kilograms. It is born with its eyes open and with a full set of milk teeth (baby teeth).

When the calf is born, the mother licks it clean. This helps to stop enemies from picking up its scent. Its chestnut brown coat has white spots and a black line running down its back. The coat blends in with the background. At about six weeks old, the calf loses its spots. A thicker, brown, fluffy coat grows to replace it.

▲ Two-day-old red deer calf

▼ Milk teeth

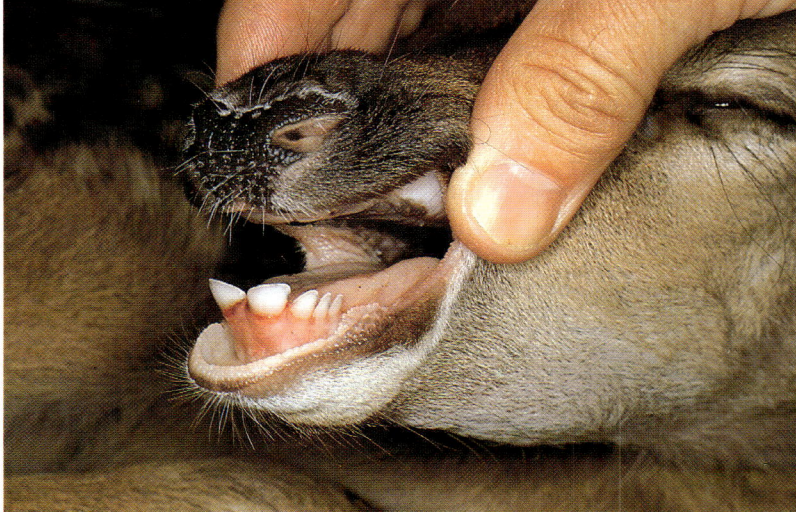

▲ Calf taking its mother's milk

▼ Young stag with its first antlers

At any sign of danger, the mother bleats. This tells the calf to lie down and keep very still. If the calf is frightened while its mother is away, it screams. The mother will run back to scare off the enemy by boxing with her front hooves.

By the end of the first day, the calf can stand and walk. In a few days, it will be able to run faster than a man. Then it is ready to rejoin the main herd with its mother. The calf drinks its mother's milk for about eight months. As it grows, it starts to feed alongside her and learns which plants to eat.

When autumn comes, the male calf has grown pedicles. It won't grow its first antler spikes until it is a year old. At two years old, the hinds drive the male calves away to join the groups of older stags.

Survival

While they are feeding, red deer are always on the look out for danger. They are very quick to notice any movement, even from a long way off. Their eyes are at the side of their heads so the deer can watch what is going on around them while they eat.

If you watch deer grazing, look at the way they twist their ears, listening for unusual sounds. They can also scent an enemy if the wind is blowing in the right direction, so make sure that the wind is blowing from the deer towards you.

▼ The leader is on the look out for danger

▲ The hinds lead their calves from danger

If a hind senses danger, she stamps her front foot to warn the herd. The herd then moves away quietly, usually running in single file. Although red deer stags have antlers and fight each other, they usually run away when there is danger.

Red deer don't have many natural enemies. In wild, hilly areas, sick calves may be taken by eagles, wild cats or foxes to feed their own young. But the main danger to red deer is man.

Red deer have always been hunted and farmed for their meat, which is called *venison*. Now laws have been passed so that deer can only be hunted at certain times of the year.

Usually, red deer live for about eight years, but they can live for up to fifteen years Sometimes they die from malnutrition because they don't have enough minerals to eat. This is why you may see blocks of salt in deer parks for the deer to lick.

Other kinds of deer

Roe deer
Height about 60 cms

Roe deer are much smaller than red deer. They are easy to recognise because of their black muzzle and white tail patch. The male roe deer is called a *buck* and the female is called a *doe*. The rut lasts from July to August and the following May, twins are born. Almost always, there is one male and one female twin. The young roe deer are called *kids*. When they are born, they have spotted coats like the young red deer calves.

A roe deer buck ▶

▼ A group of fallow deer bucks

Fallow deer
Height about 1 metre

Fallow deer have antlers which are wide and flat at the top. In summer, their coats are usually reddish-brown with large white spots and white lines running from head to tail. They can also be brown or black.

In October the herd comes together for the rut. Their young are called fawns.

Muntjac deer
Height about 40 cms

These deer are very shy and live in dense undergrowth. Muntjac deer were brought from China and India over a hundred years ago. Some escaped from the deer parks and now live in the wild.

Muntjac deer are easy to tell from other deer because of their size and because the male has tusk-shaped antlers. Muntjacs don't have a special rutting season.

▲ A muntjac buck

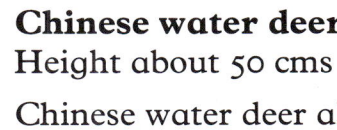

▼ A Chinese water deer

Chinese water deer
Height about 50 cms

Chinese water deer also come from China. The male Chinese water deer doesn't have antlers at all, but has very long tushes instead. The males and females come together to mate in the autumn. By June, a female Chinese water deer may have three or four *fawns*.

23

Japanese sika

Height about 1 metre

These deer, which were originally brought from Japan, are very like red deer. The main difference is that they have spotted coats. Like the red deer, the Japanese sika come together in October for the rut. The herd stays together until the spotted calves are born in May and June.

If you want to find out more about deer, there are deer Societies which collect information about deer from all over the world. But the best way to find out about deer is to visit a deer park or zoo and watch them for yourself.

Sika stags and hinds ▶

Index